THE LAMP ᴅᴀꜱᴇ

-AN ILLUSTRATED GUIDE TO LAMPS-

BY

VARIOUS

British Library Cataloguing-in-Publication Data
A catalogue record for this book is available from
the British Library

Making Lampshades

Lampshades are designed to cover light bulbs in order to diffuse the light they emit. Conical, cylindrical and other forms such as floor, desk or table-top mounted, as well as suspended lamp models are the most common, and can be made in a wide range of materials. Whilst today, lampshades serve a bigger purpose than merely dimming the glare of light bulbs - they can provide a canvas for the expression of personal, interior style; this was not always the case.

In late seventeenth century Paris, the first public lanterns, 'réverbères' made their appearance in the centre of the streets. They were oil lamps which lit the roads at night - covered with reflectors, hung above the centre of the streets. Their use soon spread to Milan, where the oil lanterns were covered by a semi-spherical reflector above the flame, which projected the light downwards, while another reflector, slightly concave and near the flame, served to direct the light latterly. This process worked reasonably well, however the introduction of 'gas light' was the innovation which necessitated shades, as opposed to reflectors. The flame, fed by gas, was intense, uniform and adjustable, white and brilliant instead of the reddish or orange of oil lamps or candles. Consequently, it had to be filtered by opal glass or light fabric shades. Lampshades were no longer used to direct the light but to attenuate it. Today, our modern electric light bulbs are no different - and the prevalence and diversification of the lampshade on every high street is a testament to its popularity.

Now, lampshades are available from almost every home furnishings store in the country. However, the only way to achieve a bespoke look, with a fabric style and colour chosen to match your room/s perfectly, is to make your own! There are three main types of lampshade, an hence construction differs substantially according to the desired outcome. But they are: 'Hard Frame', which either comes as a one piece frame or as a set of two rings (a washer top and a bottom wire ring, generally), 'Panelled Shade', which can be triangular, rectangular, square, hexagonal or bell-shaped; with vertical spokes which create the shape of pleats and panels, and 'Tailored shades', whereby the frame is measured first, and one or many different types of material are used. Hard frames are probably the simplest to make, so for the novice lampshade maker, these are the best to start with.

Making lampshades is fairly easy to do - but often hard to do neatly! Accordingly, one should leave at least an hour for the task. It does not cost a lot though, probably around twenty pounds for the kit (rings, backing material and sticky tape), plus whatever material is chosen. As a final note, fabric choice is crucial - red and yellow tones will give off a warm glow, whereas greens and blues will give off a cold light. It is also important to make sure that the fabric is not too thick or too thin, allowing the desired amount of light to escape. We hope that this book will inspire the reader to try making their own lampshades, Enjoy.

CONTENTS

Table lamp bases: Converting bottles and jars — fitting a lamp socket and switch — "Pifco" adaptor — use of a back-plate — drilling a hole for the flex — suitable drills — precautions.

MANY of the lampshades described in this book are suitable for use as covers for table lamps, and in addition to making attractive lampshades, the home handicraft worker can make many very effective bases for table lamps. A wide variety of ordinary articles can quite simply be transformed into table lamps, and some suggestions are given in Fig. 32.

Bottles and jars are favourites for conversion to table-lamp

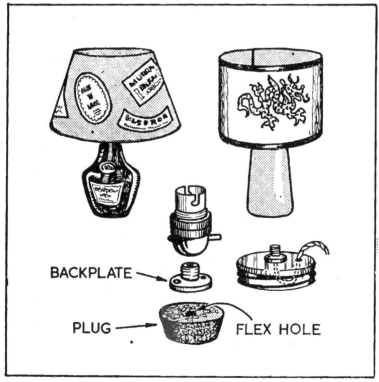

FIG. 32.   TABLE-LAMPS

bases, and other articles that may be used for this purpose include vases, candlesticks, large polished pieces of wood, and various kinds of ornaments. In most cases converting any article to a lamp base consists in fitting the object with a lamp socket and switch so that it may easily and efficiently be wired for electric current.

Converting jars and bottles, vases and ornaments with lids or necks is a fairly simple matter. This can be done by using a special adaptor made for this purpose. This is the "Pifco" adaptor, which consists of a socket to take the electric bulb and switch together as one unit, that is secured to a cork. The cork is fashioned as a roll which may be adjusted to fit most bottles with no neck. If this type of fitting is used for converting a bottle into a lampshade base, it will be necessary to make provision for fitting the flex which is attached to the lampholder through a central hole in the cork stopper. For this it will be necessary to drill a hole in the glass, and this is described later in this chapter.

Wine bottles make very attractive lamp bases, and the design motif may be emphasized by attaching labels from wine bottles to the shade, if it has a smooth cover. Parchment lends itself extremely well to this type of cover, and the labels and cover . should be given a coat of clear varnish so that they may easily be cleaned without damage.

A method of fitting wide-necked jars and bottles with a lamp-holder socket is by using what is known as a back-plate. This is illustrated in Fig. 32. The back-plate may be soldered or bolted to a metal jar cover or closure of wood or cork that has been cut to shape to fit the top of a bottle or jar. The back-plate may be screwed into the main material. If a back-plate is used the lamp socket must be of the type which is fitted with an internal thread which screws over the threaded base of the back-plate. In the case of a wide-necked jar or bottle the flex hole may be made in a closure as illustrated in Fig. 32, and the socket may be of the type fitted with a switch, or a separate "torpedo" switch may be fitted to the flex. For this type of lamp base a batten-holder type of lamp socket may be successfully used in place of the back-plate and holder.

The batten holder is attached to the closure of the jar, which may be cork, wood, or a metal lid, by bolting or screwing it in place, and if a batten holder is used it will also be necessary to make provision for the entry of the flex, so that it may be attached to the connections of the lampholder.

If the flex is to run through the lamp base it will be necessary to make a hole for this purpose. If the base is wood it will be found a simple matter to drill a hole for the flex, but if the table-lamp base is of glass, stoneware or china, it will not be quite so easy to make the necessary hole. In most towns this can be done locally by taking the base with the position of the hole marked to a hardware merchant or builders' merchant, who will very often drill glass and china at the owner's risk.

The drilling may also be done by the lampshade maker, and for this purpose special drill bits may be obtained. These may be used with the electrically powered drills or with hand drills. These special drills with hardened points are normally used for drilling holes in brick, stone, tile, marble, cement or slate, and although they are not specially manufactured for drilling glass or china-ware, they may be successfully used provided reasonable care is taken while the work is being done. In this work it is essential to ensure that a firm and even pressure is maintained while the drill is being rotated against the material.

It will be found necessary to mark the point of entry in the material to be drilled, and this can be done with the tang of a file. It is necessary to make only a very small indentation, so that the point of the drill is guided and does not "wander" as the drill is rotated.

Full details of the use of carbon-tipped drills, which are manu-factured under various trade names, may be obtained from the suppliers, and the drills are available in a very large range of sizes. For the flex of most types of lamp a $\frac{1}{4}$-in. drill will be found a suitable size.

During the drilling of glass or chinaware it is advisable to use a lubricant to prevent the tool and material from becoming over-heated. A suitable lubricant for this purpose can be made by dissolving crushed camphor in turpentine. During the work of drilling it is important to ensure that the drill is pressed firmly into the hole being cut as the drill is rotated, and the direction of the drill should not be changed. If this is done the glass or china-ware will in all probability crack or split.

Care must be taken in wiring the lamp base to ensure that the connections are properly made. The covering of the flex should not be frayed, and connections both to the adaptor and the plug should be made so that the ends of the wire are securely held and sufficient insulation is provided to prevent the two wires of the flex from touching. If the worker has no knowledge at all of electrical wiring it is advised that this be done by a competent electrician.

CHAPTER VIII

Lampshade bases: Aid to sales — use of common articles and objects — converting a vase — plug for the neck — suitable materials — shaping the plug — care in fitting — attaching the socket — another pottery base — different conversion treatment — use of back plates — drilling pottery and glass — suitable lubricant — practise — assembling the lamp base. A covered bottle — pattern — use of " **Crino-thene** " — thonged corners — finishing — assembling — light reflection. A preserve jar with moulded cover — use of " **Wallart** " — mixing and applying — drying — final coat — stippled finish — insulating the flex hole. A candle-stick lamp base made from " **Crinothene** " — fittings — making the column — heat-sealed edges — making the base — handle — wiring-up and fitting — a cord-covered base — suitable foundation — attaching the cord — decorative treatment.

QUITE a large proportion of lampshades made are for use on table lamps, and the home craftsman working for profit will appreciate that there is greater chance of sales if lampshade stands and bases are made and offered with the shades. This chapter, therefore, deals with some of the methods of making and fitting bases. A great many common articles can be utilised for lampshade bases. Such things as vases, bottles, jars, leap to mind, and if the approach to their transformation is imaginative and ingenious, these simple objects may be made worth many times their cost.

The first lampshade stand described and illustrated in Fig. 25 is a pottery vase of simple design. To make vases of this type into lampshade bases, it is necessary to fit a lamp-holder socket to the top of the article. For a vase with a wide neck, such as the one illustrated, the socket fitting may be attached to a piece of wood or cork cut to shape, to fit into the mouth of the vase. Tackle the job in the following sequence.

The materials required are a piece of wood or cork about an inch thick, a batten socket (as illustrated), to hold the lamp bulb, three one-inch screws to fit the socket to the top, some flex of suitable colour, and a torpedo switch for fitting over the flex (if desired, the switch may be incorporated in the lamp-holder socket, but the batten type sockets described are not often fitted with press switches). In addition, some strong liquid glue will be required, a pair of scissors and a screwdriver.

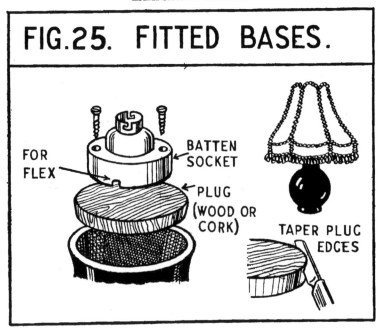

FIG.25. FITTED BASES.

FOR FLEX

BATTEN SOCKET

PLUG (WOOD OR CORK)

TAPER PLUG EDGES

The first thing to do is to cut the piece of wood or cork to shape, to fit firmly into the top of the vase. This should be done carefully as it is very easy to crack the top of a vase, if too much force is used. It is best to taper-trim the edges of the material with a very sharp knife (see Fig. 25), and finish off with glass-paper. Before fitting the shaped plug in the top of the vase, the batten socket should be attached to it. If the plug is made of wood, it is a simple matter to screw the socket into place, but if it is made of cork, it may be found that the screws may not hold very well, and if that is so, longer screws should be used through the cork and fastened into a piece of wood placed under the top—this is illustrated in Fig. 25. Before attaching the socket fitting, provision should be made for the flex. This may be fitted at the top of the plug, by removing a small piece of the side of the fitting at the bottom, or it may be fitted through a hole in the plug and brought up through another hole in the side of the plug (see the illustration). When the batten-holder has been firmly fixed in place and flex fitted, if it has to go through the top, the shaped piece should be fitted to the top of the vase. Brush liquid glue round the edge of the shaped top and inside the top of the vase. Insert the shaped top in the vase, making certain that it is firmly housed, and set the base aside for the glue to set. The lamp should be wired up after the glue has set, and the top of the plug should be treated to tone with the lampshade base. If it is considered necessary to weight the base, this should be done before fixing the top in place. Sand is suitable for weighting lampshade bases.

The next lampshade base described is also made from a pottery vase, but the conversion treatment is different from that of the first vase. The lamp socket of this lamp-base, which is illustrated in Fig. 26, incorporates a press switch, the top of the vase is smaller, and the flex is fitted through a hole drilled in the side of the vase at the bottom. First a wood or cork plug should be made to fit into the top of the vase. It should be made to fit into the top of the vase. It should fit snugly with tapered edges, and should not require any force to insert it. A hole for the flex should be drilled through the middle of the plug, and a back plate—illustrated in Fig. 26—should be fitted directly over the drilled hole. The flat base of the back plate is drilled for screwing, and it should be fitted firmly to the plug. The top of the back plate is threaded, to take the lamp-holder socket. After preparing the top, and before it is glued in place, a hole should be drilled through the pottery vase. Drilling through pottery or glass is not very difficult, providing care is taken, but it is advisable to practise first on odd pieces of pottery and glass before attempting to make a hole in a valuable piece.

A very hard drill is required for drilling glass and pottery and it should be used with a lubricant made by shredding camphor in turpentine. Before drilling, wrap a piece of cloth round the vase or bottle, and fix it carefully in a vice, or get someone to hold it for you. Mark the position of the hole, which may be started with the point of a broken file, and commence drilling. Use a high speed drill and do not exert too much pressure on the article being drilled. Use the lubricant freely and hold the drill very lightly, when it is apparent that it is about to come through the other side of the material. After drilling practise holes in odd pieces of material, the worker should have acquired the 'feel' of the operation, and be able to work on valuable pieces. After drilling the base,

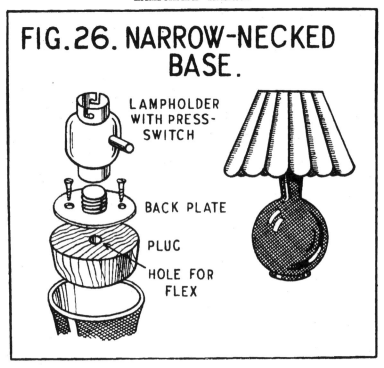

FIG.26. NARROW-NECKED BASE.

LAMPHOLDER WITH PRESS-SWITCH

BACK PLATE

PLUG

HOLE FOR FLEX

the lamp may be assembled; thread one end of a length of flex through the drilled hole and bring it out through the top of the vase. Thread the end through the hole in the plug and, leaving some to spare for fitting to the socket, tie a single knot to hold the flex in place. Brush glue round the tapered edge of the plug and inside the top of the vase, insert the plug and leave it to firmly set.

When the glue has set, untie the knot in the top end of the flex and wire-up the combination press-switch lampsocket, and screw it over the back plate. At the other end of the flex, fit a suitable electric plug. The top of the vase plug should be treated, to merge it with the colour and texture of the vase. If it is thought necessary to weight the base, it should be done before the shaped plug of wood or cork is affixed inside the top of the vase. Sand is usually used for weighting lampshade bases, but in the case of a drilled base, where the sand would be likely to trickle through the hole, some other weighting

8

material should be used. Plaster is suitable, providing a passage is left for the flex. Flex is obtainable in many colour finishes, and a suitable coloured flex should be used with lamp bases, to tone with the general colour scheme.

In Fig. 27, another type of lampshade base is shown. It is made from a bottle with square corners, which is covered with **"Crinothene"** of the same colour, or a contrasting colour to that of the lampshade cover of the same material. All kinds of bottles may be covered in this way, even if the manufacturer's name is embossed on the side of the bottle. To make a **"Crinothene"** cover for a bottle base, a pattern should first be made in stiff card. Place the bottle on a sheet of thin card, mark round the base with a pencil, and from the corners, draw pencil lines as shown in the illustration. Cut and remove the waste card and test the pattern over the bottle (see Fig. 27). The corner edges of the pattern should meet. Shape the top of the pattern to the neck of the bottle, and,

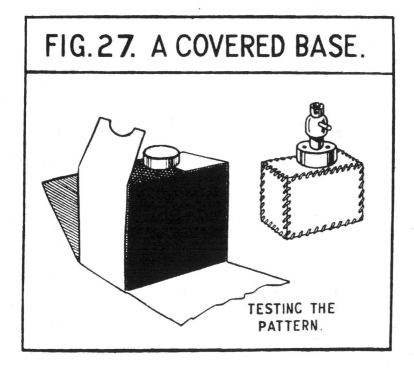

FIG. 27. A COVERED BASE.

TESTINC THE PATTERN.

when it is a perfect fit, use it for marking and cutting the "**Crinothene**" to shape. After cutting the cover to shape, punch thonging holes in each of the joining edges and make certain that the same number of holes are punched in each pair of joining edges. Drill a hole through the bottle, near the base in one side, then attach the cover. Place the bottle over the "**Crinothene**" shape and bend the sides of the material up to cover the bottle. Wind string round the sides of the cover near the top to hold it firm while thonging, and commence thonging the corners of the cover. Begin from the bottom of the corners, thong one or two holes, joining one corner, then commence fastening the other corners. Thong upwards and fasten one or two holes in each corner of the base-cover in turn. Fasten the neck firmly, knot the ends of the thonging and neatly tuck the odd ends of thonging between the cover and the glass. Cut a small hole in the cover where the glass has been drilled to permit passage of the flex, which should be of a colour to match or tone with the colour of the "**Crinothene**". After completing the cover, a back plate should be fitted to the metal screw-top closure of the jar. First pierce a hole for the flex in the centre of the top of the screw top of the bottle, remove any paint from the cap of the bottle, and solder the base of the metal back plate to the closure, making sure that the hole in the back plate is over the hole in the top of the cap. Paint the cap and the back plate to match the cover, but be careful not to clog the threads of the top of the back plate with too thick a coat of paint. After fitting the back plate, and wiring the flex to a combined switch socket-holder, which should be screwed over the back plate, the lamp is ready for use. If the jar used for the base has a fairly wide bottom, it should not be necessary to weight it, and the light from the lamp will shine into the "**Crinothene**" covered glass base, giving it a very pleasing appearance when in use.

Many other types and shapes of bottles and jars are suitable for use as lamp bases. In Fig. 28, is illustrated a preserve jar used as a foundation on which to shape a lamp-base for a bedside lamp. The material used for covering the jar is "**Wallart**", a **Winsor & Newton** product. "**Wallart**" is a white powder which, when mixed with water, forms a paste. The paste may be modelled, carved and moulded to any shape required, and is used extensively in the decoration of walls for stippled or modelled finishes. To make a lamp-base

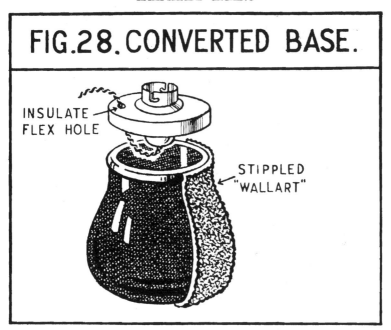

FIG.28. CONVERTED BASE.

INSULATE FLEX HOLE

STIPPLED "WALLART"

of the type illustrated, clean the jar and remove the cap. Mix **"Wallart"** with water, adding the powder to the water (full instructions are given on the packet), and spread the paste which should be mixed rather thickly, over the jar. With a broad knife or modelling tool, roughly shape the **"Wallart"** covering. Put the covered jar aside until the **"Wallart"** has hardened, and do not try to accelerate hardening by the application of heat. When the **"Wallart"** has set and is hard, it may be rubbed down with coarse glasspaper, or a coarse file, to shape. After shaping, any dust should be removed by brushing, and another coat of **"Wallart"** applied. The second coat, which is also the final coat, should not be mixed so thickly as the first coat. Apply the final coat of **"Wallart"** and stipple it. This may be done with a sponge or a stiff brush, which should be lightly tapped all over the material, while it is soft. After stippling, set the lamp-base aside for the covering to harden. When it is hard and dry, it may be coloured. A coat of size should be applied first and then the stippled cover may be painted with oil colours, being finally

D

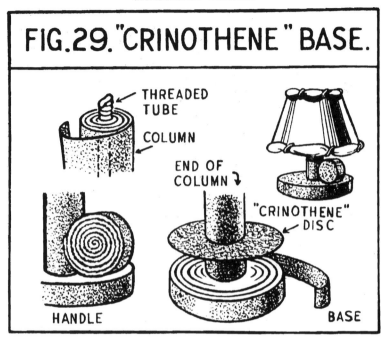

FIG.29. "CRINOTHENE" BASE.

THREADED TUBE

COLUMN

END OF COLUMN ↓

"CRINOTHENE" DISC

HANDLE

BASE

varnished. **"Wallart"** is a very useful material and may be used for many craftwork purposes. A lamp-holder should be fitted to the closure of the jar, as illustrated in Fig. 28, by cutting a hole in the metal top large enough for entry of the lamp-holder socket, which is kept in place by screwing the two parts of the socket together over the cap. A smaller hole should be cut in the metal top of the jar for the flex, and an insulating washer should be fitted, to prevent the flex becoming frayed in contact with the edges of the hole. After assembly and wiring-up, the lamp is ready for use.

"Crinothene" may be used for making lamp-bases without the addition of any other material, except the fitting. A solid **"Crinothene"** lamp-base is illustrated in Fig. 29. It is shaped in the form of a candle and candle-stick, and is quite easy to make. A metal tube is required, upon which the upright column is formed, and the tube should be threaded at one end to take a bulb-holder socket. The base may be made any size, but it would be better to make it small, rather than large, which would be out of character with the design. To make this attractive lamp-base, first obtain a five and a half inch length of tubing with a screw thread cut in one end for attachment of the bulb socket. Cut "**Crinothene**" in strips, five and a half inches wide, and for this, odd pieces may be used up, providing they are all the same colour. The strips of "**Crino-thene**" should be tightly rolled round the column support, leaving the threaded end of the tube to project at one end for about half an inch, with a recess at the other end of the roll to make a passage for the flex. Roll the strips round tightly and heat-seal the joins if odd lengths of the material are used. Make the column to a thickness of about one-and-a-quarter inches in diameter, and heat-seal the overlapping end of the "**Crinothene**" on the outside of the roll, marking it with a small heated tool to resemble the roughened surface of the material, and heat-seal the top and bottom edges of the column. Cut a "**Crinothene**" circle with a hole in it large enough to cover the top of the column completely (see the illustration—Fig. 29), place it over the top of the column and heat-seal the edges of the holed disc to the round edge at the top of the roll forming the column. Use the heated blade of a small knife and model the edges of the material carefully.

The base of the lamp-stand is made next and is also formed of strips of "**Crinothene**". These may be cut from odd pieces of material and should be from three-quarters of an inch to one inch wide. Heat-seal the end of the first strip to the base of the column and wind it round. Heat-seal all joining edges and continue rolling the narrow strips round the base of the column until it measures four-and-a-half to five inches across the base. Carefully heat-seal the final end of the roll and model it with a tool to resemble the roughened surface of "**Crino-thene**". Drill horizontally through the roll from the outside of the base to the recessed centre of the base, for the passage of flex, which is fitted after completing the lamp-base. With a broad-bladed knife, which should be heated, smooth over the underside of the circular base, joining the edges of the material and making the base smooth and even. Cut a round piece of "**Crinothene**", with a hole in the centre to fit over the column and use it to cover the top of the base. With a small heated knife, heat-seal the outside edge of this piece, to the top edge of the circular base and model the edges to conceal the join. The ring handle shown in the illustration—

Fig. 29, is built up of strips of **"Crinothene"**, heat-sealed to the column and base, and with edges heat-sealed and covered with round pieces of **"Crinothene"**. Care should be taken at every stage to ensure that the heat-sealed joints are strongly made. After making the base, it should be wired up, using flex of a suitable colour, and a press-switch socket-holder screwed over the top of the column. Many different shapes and styles of lampshades may be made by shaping and heat-sealing **"Crinothene"**, and the lampshades used with them covered with the same material, in the same colour, or a contrasting colour.

"Perspex" is suitable for use with **"Crinothene"** and other materials, for making stands and bases for lampshades, providing the material is used intelligently and the design and colouring is suitable. Many other articles and materials may be used, and the home worker will find that sales are more readily effected, if table lamps and bases are offered together. The final lamp-base described illustrates the use of a very simple material.

An ordinary jam jar with a metal closure forms the foundation of the base, which is illustrated in Fig. 30, and

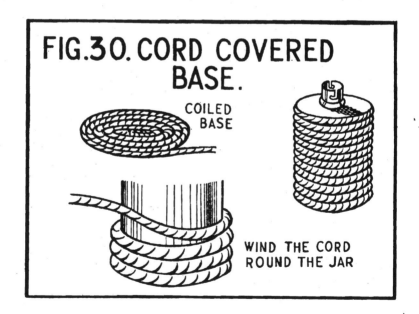

FIG. 30. CORD COVERED BASE.

COILED BASE

WIND THE CORD ROUND THE JAR

over which, sash cord is fastened. The cord is first coiled round itself to form the bottom of the lamp base, and is secured with a suitable adhesive. The cord is wound round the jar, using an adhesive on the winding and glass, to hold the cover in place, and fastened off neatly at the top of the jar, leaving room for metal snap-cap (to which a socket is fitted) to be attached. After the adhesive has set, and the base can be handled, it should be singed all over with a lighted taper, to remove any short hairs sticking out from the cord. The cover may be left plain or painted. If it is painted, one or two coats of flat white undercoating should be applied first, finishing with a coat of gloss paint or enamel. The cord motif may be repeated on the cover of the lampshade, by trimming it with silk cord of a suitable colour.

Fundamental Lamp Groups

Basically there are but three major areas from which light may reach a room: the ceiling, the walls and from somewhere within the room itself by means of "portables". In all of these areas, lighting may be installed as recessed, flush, or extending fixtures. These lights fixture forms are determined by whether they intend to supply key or spot lighting. Then too, added factors are involved whether large areas are to be covered in one thrust of the beam and whether these beams are to be soft or hard light.

In the group called ceiling pieces, light may emanate from a ceiling fixture which casts its glow directly over the surrounding surfaces or from some nearby spot set to illuminate the ceiling. These are considered high level lights both in purpose and in plan.

Pendant pieces, like chandeliers, are used especially if the ceiling level is high. Light reflected from excessive distances loses much of its potential because the unused voids between soak up so much light to little or no purpose. These pendant fixtures make it possible to bring the source closer to the area of use with greatest of economy in output and efficiency. These lighting mechanisms should serve a decorative as well as a utilitarian purpose. Their shapes, materials and color must harmonize with the architecture and the interior decoration of the room.

Wall fixtures are devices which help bring illumination to the middle areas of the room. They serve as light balances and color controls in the decoration and are made in a variety of forms.

The most permanent of these are designed as part of the architectural scheme. These are disguised within the moldings and covered with baffles so that the light achieves a directional spill over predetermined areas of the room. Cove lights are one illustration of this type of lighting.

Strip lights judiciously placed in room corners and within window cornices illustrate another method of handling wall lights. Sometimes it may suit the scheme to maintain the same source of light after sundown as before. Lights thus embedded within the window frame or arranged to produce illumination from that direction, can continue the daylight design, functions and mood.

Shadow boxes and illuminated pictures aid considerably in establishing or heightening the mood of the decoration. They can be made to bring about the focal point in the design of a group within the room.

The wall fixtures do the same thing in a more direct manner. Here the mechanical structure of the light must be designed to be in harmony with the decoration, whether traditional or modern. Another variation of this, from a mechanical point and not from one of decoration, is to set the fixture against the wall to assume as much of the flat character of the wall and become as much a part of it as possible. Then again, it may project sufficiently to add the feeling of relief sculpture yet be kept attuned to the level of the wall expanse. Thirdly, it may extend to the point where it seems and is a lamp unto itself which merely joins the wall at some logical point of the lamp design. Lanterns, brackets, sconces, spots, clip-ons or pin-ups, swivels and gooseneck lamps fall into the classification of wall lights. Special conversions like binnacle or hurricane lamps, coach and carriage lanterns or kerosene and oil lamps are further possible applications of wall light fixtures.

Where wall lights cannot project sufficiently within the room design and where accents of light are necessary to the more mobile units of decoration, the portable lamp lighting group is required. These include floor and table lamps in every form, size and construction.

Based upon specific usage, lamps will require definite sizes and shapes which will offer the required output of illumination. Lamps intended for bed use must fulfill different requirements than those planned for the desk or for the reading chair. The general illumination and the specific area coverage vary greatly in the individual departments just as they do in any combination of purposes. Similarly, the vanity light differs from the study or work lamp or the closet fixture from the garden and lawn light. Their moods are many and their color and decorative requirements are individual.

The most transient of all lamp groups used in the home are the portables. These may be exchanged, replaced or removed for many reasons. Change of season, change of fashion, of taste, mood, change of accessories or furnishings—any of these may be reason for a change.

Prominent among these are the floor lamps which are so designed and constructed as to be an independent unit in itself. Extension cords make it possible to move them about and set them up in conjunction with a variety of furniture groups. These have taken many forms during the decades of traditional interior decoration and in their electrified form they changed very little. It is surprising how many variations of the torchiere floor lamp alone there has appeared within each era of home decoration. Add to that the reflector then the shade and you have innumerable elements added to the possibilities of combination and variation.

The smaller cousin to the floor lamp is the table model. These vary considerably in height. No matter how tall or short they might be, the overall height of the lamp and the object upon which it stands should add up to the overall height of a floor lamp—a height which permits a person to stand or set near it, whichever most suits the grouping, yet avoids having the lamp light strike the eyes directly. Thus we see a highboy and a desk lamp are both short while dresser and night stand lamps are made taller. End table and dressing table lamps are quite a good deal higher than the others only because they set upon lower pieces of furniture and their overall height must maintain a predetermined level.

Basically the lamp is made up of just three major sections: the base, the shaft, and the shade. Each of these sections may be comprised of one or more parts depending upon its function and the design of the lamp.

To begin with, the *shade* covers such parts as the shade, the reflector, the bulb, and the necessary accompanying hardware. The *base* includes the support, the clamp-on part and balancing pieces. These are determined by whether the lamp attaches itself to the ceiling, clings to the wall, rests on a table or stands on the floor's surface. The *shaft* is that part which joins the other two in either flexible or rigid "weldlock". This shaft may be long or short depending upon whether it must reach from table height or floor to eye level, above or below it. Additional parts added to its functions like swivels, extensions, telescoping arms, goosenecks, brackets, clip-on or counterweights are optional and are therefore added or omitted from the design and construction of the lamp as required.

17

Lamp design follows one of two trains of creative planning. It is either devised to fit the limitations of traditional periods of decoration or the problem is approached from the pure functional angle and it parts company completely with the period styles.

Very often "Traditional-Modern" is spoken of as an arbitration between both style groups. This appeasement is hardly feasible since "Traditional" approaches the problem from the point of decorative treatment, whereas "Modern" solves its problems functionally and stops right there.

To carry either one beyond its own conventional limitations, is to make mockery of the essence of the purpose and of the point of approach. Its mongreloid results can only be labeled by approximation in appearances, not by any functional period approach to lamp design which requires the limitation set upon the forms and materials employed used during that era and adapted to the electrification of present day technology.

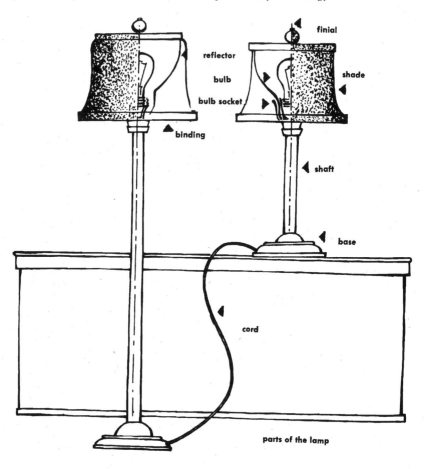

parts of the lamp

Methods of Wiring, Tying, Binding

We know that a circuit is the complete route which current must travel from its source to the mechanism which it must feed. This route is delineated with wires which carry the current to its destination. Most commonly the seat of such current is an outlet of some type into which an extension wire is plugged to continue the path of the current to the lamp light itself.

Often, intervening between the source and the ultimate point of use, electrical devices are installed for special reasons. Sometimes, they are switches, sometimes fuses, sometimes rheostats or dimmers may be another outlet for a minor circuit.

These are double wires and each made up preferably of the multiple strand rather than the single wire variety. Each wire must be insulated. This will vary with the purpose of each kind of wire. Electric lamp wire will carry a smaller load than will a heating unit. Hence, a light—perhaps cotton insulation is necessary for the lamp while the heating cord requires an asbestos wrapping for its protection.

The average length of wire appendages which are attached to a portable lamp are about ten to fifteen feet long. These only vary with the exception. Extension wire longer than that shouldn't be necessary. An outlet nearer to the source is preferable. Extension wires should not be too long either. It presents a safety hazard and should be shortened to have only as much slack as is normally required to move the lamp to all sections of its own grouping. Otherwise it should be plugged into an outlet closer to the group.

All electric currents are basically alike. They only vary in the way they flow through the line. For instance, a continuous flow in which the direction is constant and does not vary in its amount of flow at any given instant is called CONTINUOUS CURRENT, whereas a similar current moving in one direction but whose current strength rises and falls, is known as a PULSATING CURRENT. Actually, any current created by a

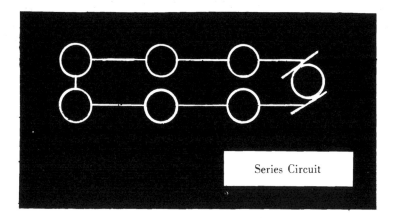

Series Circuit

19

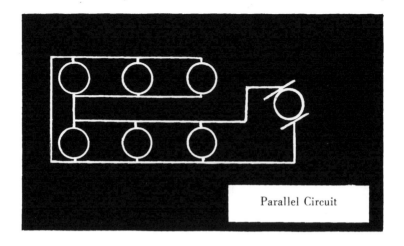

Parallel Circuit

generator is pulsating, but one which flows in a steady direction is known as DC CURRENT, but one which produces an electric current in which the flow reverses itself at fixed intervals is called AC CURRENT. OSCIL-LATING CURRENT is another form of AC current in which the flow diminishes from its maximum strength until it stops entirely. The frequency of such rise and fall of the flow is inconceivably big, often running into millions of complete oscillations each second. This varies from the INTERRUPTED CURRENT in which the circuit itself is made and broken at given and steady intervals. This type of current is used for sign flashers.

100 volts approximates one ampere charge, hence each 100 watt lamp takes about 1 ampere. Thickness of wire is measured in gage. Solid wire is very apt to break with much handling; stranded wire can withstand a great deal more. An electric current is produced either mechanically as in a generator or chemically as in a wet or a dry cell battery.

When a current passes through wires and pieces of electrical apparatus which are so connected that the current must move from one to another in turn, it is said to be wired in *series*. If, however, such current is divided two or more branches and passes through all of these at the same time, this is said to be set up in *parallel*.

In a Series Circuit, the current remains the same at each point in the circuit. Each lamp receives as great a charge as every other lamp. However, if one lamp is removed, the current is prevented from continuing through and the circuit is considered broken. In the Parallel Circuit, each branch of the circuit receives such part of the total current delivered to the combination as it needs for its function. The sum of these minor currents must equal the total current delivered. No unused portion can be stored. The excess will merely be distributed to all branches and may overcharge or burn out the electrical mechanism.

Unlike the flow of water, the flow of electricity demands a closed path. This path travels from its source of generation to its point of use and back again. It is to be assumed throughout that this flow moves in the direction from the positive (+) terminal of the battery or the generator back to the negative (—) terminal.

20

Lamp Styles in Review

From the time the cave man carried a burning faggot and lit a fire on the floor in the center of his cave domicile to a period quite recent in our growth of civilization, there was no way of making light anything but a *point* of illumination. As these faggots became oil torches, candle sconces, then gas jets, they still remained single points of brilliance which radiated more or less light depending upon the ingenuity of the pattern arrangements of reflecting surfaces surrounding it. Similarly, the central lighting fixture which was the 17th Century's contribution to diffused lighting was a concentration of a great many candles hung in the middle of the room on a tremendous fixture. As a source of illumination it was more efficient than the wall bracket since the center of the room is much more the center of man's activity than the walls. The detached lamp, an offspring of the portable torch of old, is today an infinitely better lighting solution because its position as a light source may fulfill the requirements dictated to it by its associated furniture. Its very portability enhances its flexibility and scope of usage.

Reviewing the efforts of the designers and craftsmen of the past should help us to determine to a great extent basic lines, units of design, motifs and techniques of decoration, typical materials and generally accepted lamp pieces commonly used in the Traditional Periods of the past. But this can easily be used as a guide for the present selection.

The most important movements of furniture and furnishing was developed in just a few of the eminent countries of the world. The others either imitated or adapted these forms for their own convenience and taste. England, France and America were among the more important of these. At certain periods of civilized history, Spain, Italy, the Dutch and others made their mark felt.

The attributed dates are generally very arbitrary, for styles of decoration are born long before they attain the recognition of maturity and continue to exist long after their loss of pre-eminence and the dateline of their official obituary. National and political boundaries are hardly a guarantee of the physical limits of a style. Often, there exist many cross-influences which tend to ignore man-made borders and devious routes of contact which defy any restricting enclosures. The year, 1925, marks the approximate, official beginning of the "Modern Style". Because of the strong, geometric cross-influences and imitations, it resulted more as an *international* style than a *national* one.

A history of lamp styles, as we now know it, is practically non-existent before the advent of the electric light in 1887, unless we stretch the definition of the word "lamp" to include all forms of illumination like the oil lamp, the candle and the incandescent gas mantle. Under this set of circumstances, it is virtually impossible to obtain an authentic period, electric lamp. The closest one can hope to get is an adaptation of some piece which may be closely allied to some preconceived notion of what an electric lamp should have looked like in that period of design or adapt and convert a standard piece of period accessory to serve as a "period lamp". All of this would normally fall under the heading of the Traditional Style.

In direct opposition to this philosophy of Lamp Decoration lies the Functional Modern with transitional group which grew out of the half-way thinking. The International Exposition of Decorative Arts in 1925 evoked tremendous interest in the various schools of design operating in Europe. The tendency ran in two schools; one, designated as the Romantic offering handsomely conceived forms strongly reminiscent of traditional forms, now developed into the "Traditional Modern"; the other, a social-engineering concept based upon "form which follows function", now recognized as the "Functional Modern". The latter was a natural out-growth of the social, economic and ideological changes brought about by our rapid 20th Century scientific development and technological growth. New materials and new techniques brought about new horizons. The fundamental concept of good materials, honestly expressed with fine craftsmanship of undisguised form influenced by function, stood out above all poetic obscurantism. This feeling spread throughout the continent, enveloped world art thought, and developed nationalistic trends along the way. It was based uniformly upon the naturalistic approach rather than stemming from the classical. The Bauhaus schools of Europe were vital factors in crystallizing artistic thought in this new direction.

In America, we still clung to the Traditional styles, sparked by manu-facturer to copy, and unskillfully at that, of the major historical styles with their misadapted historical motifs. Not until such iconoclasts as Louis Sullivan and Frank Lloyd Wright showed the amazing potentialities of the new age of steel, did we recognize this new external expression to have grown to adult size and importance. Not until two decades have passed have we given them the recognition due them, for at that time the commercial classicism was far too strongly entrenched. It took this length of time for homes to change in architectural function to require functional furniture and furnishings. It also took several world wars and their sub-sequent reconstruction to knit these world-wide elements into a universal style.

The simple, undecorated utilitarian form is adequately beautiful, if designed with an honest respect for the materials and the new conveniences that have come to serve our needs. In accordance with these special condi-tions, it becomes the logical conclusion that we design these implements of our everyday use to serve us best under those conditions. So too, does lighting by electricity create new problems and expose new possibilities. We should, therefore, wisely discard the technique of lighting by "elec-trified-candles and kerosene" and redesign according to these new ideas and possibilities. Thus the nature of the materials have become far more important than the designer's attempt at creating an aesthetic form in the established sense. The basic sense of beauty is achieved when the objects are designed precisely to their required use, their final forms being no more than the expression of this use and of the natural possibilities of the materials of which they are made. Non-essential ornament is dropped off like over-ripe apples.

Rooms cease to be regarded as the interior of a box. They are, rather, treated backgrounds and continuities of precise and enclosed activities. The furniture becomes more closely integrated with the walls, floors, ceil-ings, etc. Artificial lighting, ventilation, seating, sleeping, movements, eating and other elements of human occupancy become essential factors for artistic-functional conception and decoration.

23

Materials for the Lamp Base

In the strictest sense of the word, there is no such thing as any one or another material most suitable for use as a lamp base. Almost any one material or combination of materials may be used. It depends for the most part on what form that material takes and to what purpose it is put. One may be more suitable from the point of view of texture, another from the standpoint of weight, a third may be more desirable for its color or even its strength. Material for the lamp base is chosen for its functional suitability, its physical and mechanical adaptability to supply the lamp needs, and for its aesthetic affinity to the style for which it is planned and the group in which it is expected to fit. These are the interlocking and overlapping areas which will determine the selection.

Even with this guide in view, one may arrive at several equally good selections. Personal taste is then an obvious factor. Involved with this is the limitation of materials called for by some who wish to adhere strictly to a particular traditional style and the possible availability of that material imposed by economic or geographic limitations. Let us scan the more common materials likely to be available and examine the varied forms in which they may be procurable.

First, there are the *ceramic* materials. These may vary from the rough, unglazed brick-like clays to the very delicate porcelains. There are many different kinds of clays, each, when fired, producing a different kind of "biscuit"—different in color, different in texture, different in strength. These may be glazed in many ways, the colors of the glazes depending upon the location of manufacture, place of import of glazing materials, and the technique used. These have been known to differ within the same locality in England, Germany, Italy or France because one locality may import its technicians or materials while the other utilizes its local talent.

To further complicate such choice, these same materials, techniques and craftsmen may produce a variety of forms, all adaptable to lamp base use. Statuary, pottery, geometric blocks and tiles are all possibilities as lamp bases; size, form, color and finish will determine to which purpose or place it is applicable. This material may require the addition of a base plate or some other device to add greater weight to secure stability for the lamp.

The choice of *wood* exposes a new realm of materials suitable for lamp base use. Here, too, the form will determine to a large extent, the kind of wood to be selected and the method by which it should be made. Suppose we choose solid wood planks. Geometric forms may be hewn from one relatively heavy piece of wood or else built up by assembling several thinner boards to construct the plinth, box or sphere. Full sculptural pieces will naturally require solid blocks of wood, whereas low-relief carving may employ pieces of lesser thickness. Piercing, underlays and even marquetry appliques may easily be used on thin panelling. Veneers are used mainly when an entire flat surface is to be covered with a thin film of wood to improve its color, grain and/or texture. Space forbids a complete explanation on the nature, types and techniques of woods. Suffice to say that a lamp base must have sufficient bulk to support the upper structure which is, of course, an integral part of the lamp itself.

Metal offers a variety of forms to the lamp base designer. While one metal may weigh more than another, be of a different color than the other, they are all manufactured in many similar forms. They come in sheets of assorted thicknesses (gauges) and sizes; as tubes of all diameters with a variety of wall thickness; as wire of all shapes like round, half-round, square, hexagonal, etc., and in many gauge thicknesses; as rods of the wire shape, but over one-quarter inch in diameter; of screening mesh woven from wire; as blocks and ingots from which castings are made; as special forms preshaped in the punch press or the stamping machine. These are only the raw forms in which they may be purchased to be worked on. Since metals differ chemically, they are bound to have physical properties which are more desirable for one reason or another. Color may vary, weights of metals are not alike, tensile strength, malleability, costs and working properties differ to such an extent as to make one metal more desirable than another for use in a particular lamp.

Some metals tarnish, covering the metal surface with a mellow color. Some receive coatings which are undesirable. These are the "patina" coloring which may be achieved either in due time and exposure, or may be hurried along by chemical persuasion. Techniques like anodizing of aluminum, metal plating, of one metal over the base of another to improve the whole or part of the surface for practical or aesthetic reasons, fall under the same type of technique as patina coloring.

In addition, the methods of adding surface decoration runs the whole gamut of metal techniques invented by man through the centuries. Etching, engraving, damascening, chasing, soldered or brazed appliques, enameling, piercing, stamping, punching, riveting, lapidary and the vast variety of abrasive finishes are just some of the decorative means at the craftsman's call with which to work on metal.

Plastic, the most recently popularized material, serves as a very adequate source from which to select and construct lamp bases. This material has distinctly individual properties, yet within its own sphere may vary greatly one from the other. All "plastics" are not alike, neither in color, weight, tensile or ductile strength, insulation and conductivity properties, nor in workability. In the main, all plastics fall into two basic divisions, the thermoset and the thermoplast, the latter of which covers most of our synthetic plastics. The *thermoset* group are those plastic materials which, in their process of manufacture, have been "fixed" and hardened by means

of heat and like scrambled eggs once fried, no amount of additional heat will cause them to soften. While the *thermoplast* materials, on the other hand, can be brought to a solid state with the addition of heat, can be re-softened later by the addition of "wet or dry" heat, whichever it may require.

These plastic materials are manufactured in many forms; sheets, rods, tubes, bars, film, fibers and extruded forms of the molding stripe. Whether fashioned from one piece or fabricated out of many, plastic lamp bases have to overcome their lack of weight which is so desirable toward the stability of a lamp.

There are in addition, the powdered and liquid forms of plastics which may be cast like plaster and "cured or set" under special conditions. This material ranges from the transparent kind, colorless or stained, in which various things may be embedded, to the full opaque kind, white or colored, which may be used in every way plaster of paris can, with the added advantage of having a harder, tougher material which can be polished to a much higher gloss. With this, preformed parts are possible as are decorative sculptured cap and base pieces, incised or low-relief modelled switch plates, etc.

The classifications of *rock*, more commonly accepted as stone by the layman, offers the lamp base maker a vast number of different materials which may be turned to advantage. In the *igneous rock* group we find the large family of granites so very popular with stone sculptors. Without involved detail, we can readily see that large, simple lamp bases easily adaptable to geometric or carved forms, are conceivably constructed from this type of material. There is no doubt that the stone-carving technique involved in this is a slow, painstaking process, but the end result is without any doubt a strong, durable and attractive lamp. The granite is available in many tones in the gray and tan families sprinkled with assorted colors of many minerals and ranging from a finely dispersed grain to a rather heavy sand-like effect. These may be polished to a very high luster or left matt-finished. The finest examples may be seen on tombstones. Then, of course, there is the volcanic glass, the obsidian, so popular with the Egyptian sculptors.

The *metamorphic rock* includes, in the main, the marble and the sandstone groups, the more popular of the two being the first. This runs the spectral gamut of white, cream-colored, the green, the gray and the red families. Adding to their beauty and interest, they come in the fairly uniform colors and range through the variated and veined markings. Marble can be polished to an exceedingly high luster. Some, like alabaster, are soft enough to be turned on a lathe. Softer still are the soapstones which can practically be whittled with a knife. These are available in tones of gray and in white highly tinted. Some have streaks and markings closely resembling their harder cousins, the marbles. These make interesting lamp bases.

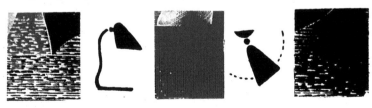

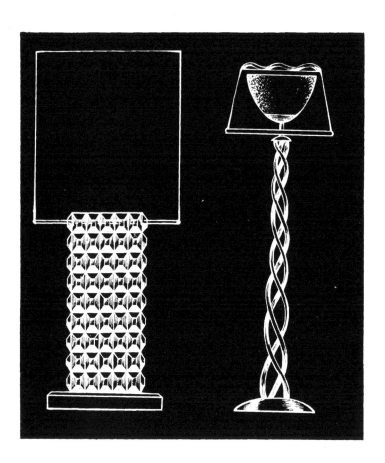

METAL			
BASIC AVAILABLE SHAPES	FORMING METHODS	DECORATIVE TECHNIQUES		FINISHING METHODS

BASIC AVAILABLE SHAPES	FORMING METHODS	DECORATIVE TECHNIQUES		FINISHING METHODS
Sheet	Hammering	Anodizing	Repoussé	Polishing
Rod	Sawing	Planishing	Damascene	Buffing
Bars	Filing	Piercing	Plating	Antiquing
Ingots	Bending	Chasing	Enameling	Matting
Tubes	Cutting	Soldering	Stipling	Texturing
Cast forms	Drilling	Riveting	Punching	Lacquering
Pressed or stamped	Machining	Engraving	Stamping	Waxing
preforms	Casting	Etching	Inlaying	
Wire	Grinding			
	Soldering			
	Brazing			
	Welding			
	Riveting			

The *sedimentary* family of *rocks* provides us with the limestones and the soap stones in a variety of reds, tans and grays for the latter and in a range from white to black for the former.

In a limited selection, the *quartz* and *crystal* group may be adapted to use in the lamp base. Because these minerals are in the gem classification, they, obviously, come in smaller pieces, are of rarer vintage and certainly more expensive. The Orientals used these minerals with judicious taste as inlays or as small, sculptured medallions applied to other materials. Polish and luster are an important part of the attraction of these gem materials. There are examples of urns, vases and statuary pieces made of quartz and crystal made during past eras which have the potentiality and promise of comfortable conversion into lamp bases.

While dwelling on the stone products, it might be well to examine the materials closely resembling this group, the plasters and the cements. *Plaster of Paris* is a white, flour-like material which, when mixed with water hardens into a smooth solid mass. This may be cast into a mold of any pre-desired shape or formed into a conveniently sized block, then carved, whittled, filed or scraped into some form fitted as a lamp base. Plaster of Paris is basically white, but may be tinted or strongly colored with the addition of dry pigment or water paint during the plaster mixing process.

To overcome its surface softness and brittleness, it may be impregnated with a plastic material used for that purpose—Plaspreg. This has its limitations in that its color is then limited to a tan, a light brown or a mahogany blackish-brown. In the light tan process, color pigments added might help to supply some desired color. However, that color must of necessity be limited by a tannish overtone. Keene cement, which is "spent plaster" offers the greatest potentialities for interesting results in that field.

Other cements, of the more common outdoor variety, offer limited results of texture and limited colors of grayish cast. Its very character suggests larger and coarser forms. It does compensate by supplying stronger body materials.

Glass is very versatile and should not be overlooked nor underestimated as a lamp base material. Many fabricated forms such as glass, brick, heavy opal and marbleized glass plate and variegated plate glass are commercially available and can be fabricated or adapted to serve as lamp base forms. Then, too, there are many complicated forms which have been factory cast, blown or ground like statuary replicas, assorted and interesting bottles and glass balls and blocks which can be made to serve that purpose. Much of the sheet glass can be cut to size and, if of the right glass, be heated and bent to shape.

Decoratively, glass has a wide latitude too. It may be faceted and polished to gem-like reflection and serve as cut-glass. It may be decorated in two tones; polished and clear, against dull and gray. There are several

methods of accomplishing this. Gray carving with a grinding wheel is one, etching with hydrogen fluoride another, and wearing off the polished surface with emery dust blasting a third. When such glass is converted into a mirror, the surfaces become multiply attractive because of the colorful reflections it adds. Such mirrors may be of silver, gold or bronze coloration, whichever is preferred. While this is accomplished by plating the metal on the underside of the glass, it can look vastly different when plated on the front surface. This can be controlled to cover restricted or designated areas. Colored enamel paints may be used as an overlay like plating. This, however, is more likely to chip off, but it does add the entire scope of color for tone and design.

We are prone to overlook the use of *paper* as a purposeful material. When shredded into a pulp-like material, prepared for and cast into a mold or modeled, it becomes as useful as wood. What it lacks in grain and texture, it makes up in its flexibility and adaptability. Sheets of paper of interesting design and special textures may be laminated as veneers over other materials. Heavier cardboards may be cut and fabricated much like wood or sheet plastic material can function equally as well. It can be made into very rigid, strong, and durable bases, to stand up to constant, hard usage and show as little wear as most of its contemporary materials. By impregnation with plastics, plaster of Paris, gums like shellac, varnish and lacquers, paint and others, too numerous to mention. The advantageous part of using this material is that it may be decorated with all the techniques used on paper of all kinds, on wood, some of those employed on plastics when impregnated with it. It may be electroplated or coated with metal-leaf to resemble that material. Paper also has the versatility of assuming molded forms when it is mached over some sculptured surface or modelled out of paper pulp. Duplication of lamp parts or decorative units are entirely feasible by casting replicas out of the pulp material. Where the lamp requires greater stability, it can be acquired by properly designing it with a low center of gravity or by weighting the base.

Another very popular and decorative medium for lamps is *leather*. Since it can only be produced in sheet or film form, it can hardly become a structural material for the lamp base. It makes, however, very excellent cover-over surface decoration. The entire field of color and a vast coverage of textural qualities can be gotten from leather. This runs from the hairy hide with its identifying textures to the characteristic skin grains peculiar to each individual kind of leather. In some cases the leather is accepted for its inherent beauty of tone and texture, but some leathers may be further enhanced with added design. General or spot dyeing and painting seems an obvious method of treating the leather. Most of these techniques involve brushing the coloring matter on pre-planned places to create illustrative or formalized decoration.

Where strong color and pattern might become the goal and painting it on not desired, piercing or punching these designs and backing them

29

up with contrasting leathers can fill the requirement. Overlays or paste-on units pattern is an excellent alternate for piercing. In either method you get a low-relief or carved effect. Use a rubber based cement to unite the many smaller pieces to each other and to its background.

Should such strong effects be out of place, leather tooling can be substituted. Not all leathers can be accommodated to this application of surface decoration. Tooling is a form of low relief modeling of the leather, pressing some areas down flatter than others with a hard tool. This is sometimes called "blind tooling." Where metal-leaf is pressed into the design, it is referred to as "gold-leaf," "silver-leaf," "bronze-leaf," "aluminum-leaf," etc., designs.

A variation of pressing the design into the leather is to burn it in with very warm or a hot marking or stamping tool. This instrument might be heated over an open flame or might be a self-heating or electrified tool much like the common soldering iron with its tip shaped to some desired form. This, too, may be done "blind" or with "metal-leaf."

A protective covering of leather lacquer, varnish, even rubbed oil or wax is advocated to preserve the leather surface against dirt, abrasion, marring and general deterioration of time and atmospheric changes. This permits handling the leather in the normal routine of use and household care of cleaning.

Perhaps the largest and certainly the most common method of creating bases is by *converting* various items like vases, urns, candlesticks, figurines, canisters, sconces, kerosene lamps and so forth. There is no limitation to this type of lamp base. Here, the size of the object chosen to serve becomes the controlling factor in selecting the lampshade and all other decorative elements. Of course, the choice of such "base object" made, in the first place, has probably been made on the basis of fitness of form, decoration and color. Where one of these elements is inadequate, it may be corrected. Such applied therapy as might be required when converting a canister may involve a new paint job to hide the commercial appearance, its advertising and other "tags." It may require a veneer of other material such as linoleum marquetry, paper montage, glass veneering, textile upholstery, metallic facading, plastic pasteovers, etc. Some of these convertibles are adaptable entoto, others require subtraction, addition or combination with other forms. This is especially true when the selected piece is too large for its intended use or when too small. In the latter case, one may use two such items like two glass blocks or combine it with some mated or compatible object. The big problem then becomes a matter of technical solution—how to tie these together without damage and without attracting attention to the means rather than the forms themselves.

The range of choice for such lamp bases are legion and each suggests its own and varied means of adaption and decoration. The field is wide open.

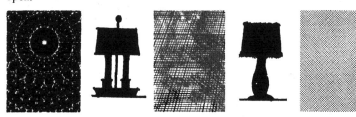

Printed in Great Britain
by Amazon